Waiting on the Rain

Conquering Everyday Challenges

By:
Fredrick R. Bailey

Zechariah 4:10 NLT
"Do not despise these small beginnings, for the LORD rejoices to see the work begin…"

Waiting
on the
Rain

Conquering Everyday Challenges

By:
Fredrick R. Bailey

All scriptures were taken from the Holy Bible, King James Version, the New International Version and New Living Translation.

Copyright © 2011
All rights reserved

Expanded Edition - 2013

Published By
Brentwood Publishers Group
www.BrentwoodBooks.com
1-800-334-8861

Dedication and Special Thanks

I dedicate this book to my lovely grandmother and grandfather, who I love dearly and miss so much!

Writing my first book was a true challenge and a great number of people had to do a lot of work in supporting me. I'd like to thank Judy Agerton, Wanda Scarborough, and Catherine Broussard for sponsoring this book. A thank you goes out to my friends who read sections of this book along the way, you know who you are.

I would also like to express my sincere appreciation to Mrs. Cindy Bryant who stepped into my life at a time when I needed her most, who became a mother figure to me and will always hold a special place in my heart. Mr. and Mrs. Garfield Duckett, thank you for believing in me, you are an amazing couple who also stepped into my life when I needed a family. A thank you goes out to Mrs. Tina Duckett and Ms. Carol Lewis for inspiring me with a great title. Many thanks to Communities In Schools for their vision to inspire great change in the lives of students across the country.

I am grateful for all of the teachers, counselors and staff members at Callaway Middle and Callaway High Schools. They believed in me and never gave up, even when I wasn't the best behaved student. Thanks to Destiny Worship Center International, whose members supported me and continually serve as a blessing in more ways than one. Also to my pastor, Christopher L. Evans Sr., for being there for me through the good and bad, who took time to talk with me and who helped develop me into the man I am today.

A very special personal thank you goes out to my family and friends including my uncles, aunts, and all of my brothers and sisters for influencing me in some way or another. To my parents; I love you all so much, words cannot explain how I feel. I am so grateful to have the best parents in the world and I would not trade you all for anything in the world. I am also grateful to my "other" parents Jerome and Regina Cofield, and their sons Maurice and Marquize, who allowed me to spend a night in their home that turned into six years. Never once did they tell me or suggest that I needed to go back home to my parents. They scarified so much so that I could have a place to lay my head and have food on the table. I love you all so much and thank you for everything you have done for me.

The thoughts and views expressed in the contents of this book are strictly those of the author.

Table of Contents

Introduction 6

Chapter 1   Entering the World 8

Chapter 2   I Had Better Days..........................14

Chapter 3   The Dark..22

Chapter 4   The Bucket 28

Chapter 5   Born Again 34

Chapter 6   The Cofields..................................41

Chapter 7   Graduating From High School.....50

Chapter 8   Statistics 62

Chapter 9   What I'm Up to Now 71

Introduction

Wow! I can't believe I'm writing my first book. A child who had to overcome many obstacles in his life is writing his first book. I'm not famous nor am I a celebrity. I'm not writing this book to become wealthy. I'm writing this book so that it will touch the lives of many people, young and old. After looking back over my life, I realize I have a story to tell. Everyone may not be able to hear me tell it, but now they can read it. I have shared my story at churches, non-profit organizations and schools. So now it's time to share it with the world.

In this book, I will share with you certain events that would shape and mold my life forever. Events that I never thought I would have made it through but because of the hand of God on my life, I made it. You will read about different moments in my life that I have gone through, and you will see how God intervened and made what was meant for bad into something that worked out for my good.

Have you ever wondered why on earth you were created? Well I did. In this book you will read why. Everyone goes through trials and tribulations, but it doesn't matter because God can turn it around. If He did it for me, surely He can do it for you in just a matter of seconds. Yes, we are going to have problems, but trust in God. He will do what His word says. God is a faithful God and will see you through any situation. Always remember the battle is already won because of what Jesus did on the cross more than two thousand years ago. In this book, you will see how God has blessed me in mighty ways. It doesn't matter what you look like, where you're from, who your parents are, or what has happened to you. There is still a bright future waiting for you in Christ Jesus. So lift up your head and be strong, for the Lord will see you through.

Chapter One

Entering the World

I was born on June 30, 1987, at Grady Memorial Hospital in Atlanta, Georgia. Once I was older, family members began to refresh my memories about my past; one that I would never want another child to face. But every person has something in their past that they wish they didn't have to go through, it's a part of life.

I was told that my mother and father met through my paternal grandfather. He was the only granddad I have ever known. My granddad was dating a lady whose sister just happened to be my mother. So to break it down, my dad and my grandfather were dating sisters at the same time. A little funny isn't it? As time passed, my dad traveled from LaGrange, Georgia, to Atlanta to work with my granddad and to see my mom. But in the process, my dad had a girlfriend who lived in LaGrange, who became my stepmom. But I have always referred to and saw her as my mother because for many years that's all I knew.

As my dad continued to travel back and forth to Atlanta, he continued to see my mom and eventually became pregnant with me, her fifth child. Around the same time mom was pregnant, my stepmother back in LaGrange was also pregnant, but she had a miscarriage a couple of months later. My stepmom had two children of her own, a son and daughter; both older than me. A couple of weeks after my birth, mom decided that she couldn't take care of me anymore since having five children was such a burden at a young age. My mother called my father so he could take me to live with him in LaGrange. After hearing this story as a young person, I started to think more about life and why I really didn't get the opportunity to grow up with my biological sisters and brothers. I am proud of the fact that my father took responsibility for his actions and came to Atlanta to bring me back to LaGrange.

LaGrange

While heading back to LaGrange, my dad had to think of a valid reason to explain bringing a newborn baby home. He knew this would hurt my stepmom, especially after she just had a miscarriage. Once in LaGrange, dad placed me on the front porch of their house where he lived with my stepmom, her children and my grandmother. Being very nervous and afraid, my dad rang the doorbell and left me alone on the front porch while he went to hide behind a tree in the yard. My stepmom came to the door and saw the "most handsome baby ever" sitting there in a car seat. According to her, she knew instantly that I was my dad's child. Because she is a warm-hearted person, she picked me up and took me inside the house. My dad waited to see if she would call the police but she never did. Later that day, my dad went back home to face reality. Surprisingly, she wasn't angry and she wasn't unwilling to accept me in her family. She always told me that she knew this baby belonged to my dad when she saw how long my head was. Even though she wasn't really upset with my dad, I can imagine the kind of pain, hurt, and distrust my stepmother must have felt, when she discovered the man she loved brought home a child he had with another woman.

Jeremiah 1:5 KJV

"Before I formed thee in the belly I knew thee, and before thou camest forth out of the womb I sanctified thee, and I ordained thee a prophet unto the nations"

I used this scripture here because of the meaning it has in my life. Many people grow up not knowing why they were born and sometimes they don't want to go on living. I am here today to say that you were born for a reason and that God is also with you. He will not leave you nor forsake you. God knew you while you were in your mother's womb and he had a plan for you even before you were born. So don't get upset and say things like "I wish I was dead", or "I wish I was never born." We are not mistakes, in fact we have a purpose in this world and we will do great things in our lifetime. We are children of Christ.

Taking By Force

As I was getting older, around 4 or 5 years of age, my granddad had a birthday party in Atlanta, and my dad took me with him to the party. From this point on, I can remember everything that ever happened in my life. Once again, my granddad was dating my aunt and they lived together in Atlanta. My mother and her entire family were present at this party. Being at the party, I wasn't really comfortable around this side of the family because I didn't know who they were.

I remember being inside of the house while my dad was in front of the house laughing and talking to family and friends. As I was sitting on the floor, one of my mother's brothers picked me up and held me in his arms. After a moment or two, my uncle started to, my uncle started to walk outside of the house with me still in his arms and suddenly I began to notice that he was picking up speed and running towards the back of the house and darted into the woods. At that moment, I began to cry out for my dad but once he heard what was happening we were too far away for him to catch us. I remember seeing him but it was too late, my uncle was on the side of a major interstate, where a black two door car was waiting for us. My uncle placed me in the arms of my mom, and then she placed me in the back seat of the car and we took off.

My dad didn't have a chance to catch us. I was scared and cried until I couldn't cry any longer. I really didn't know what was going on and was in shock. I couldn't believe this was happening to me. We pulled up to one of my mother's friend's houses, got out of the car and went inside. We went to the kitchen and sat down at the table. They poured me some orange juice and sat it in front of me. I sat there thinking over and over, "Why is this happening to me?" I was truly sad and wanted to be with my dad and stepmom. I finally took a sip of orange juice and dropped my head on the table, wishing that I was dreaming.

Reflections

Discuss what to do when you encounter things that you don't like and why things are happening that you don't think are fair.

_____
_____
_____
_____
_____
_____
_____
_____
_____
_____
_____
_____
_____
_____
_____
_____
_____
_____
_____
_____
_____
_____
_____
_____
_____

Discuss how you can turn a negative situation into a positive situation and review learning experiences.

___

Have students do self-assessment and help them understand that an important point in life is how you conduct yourself and react under pressure.

Evaluate interests, attributes, goals, innate abilities (i.e. I enjoy ___, I dislike___, I value, I fear, my talents are, I'm known for my, I'm proud of, I see myself as, others describe me as, my strengths are, my weaknesses are, I need to work on).

___

Chapter 2

I Had Better Days

I woke up the next morning with a broken heart and very confused because I still didn't know what was going on. I knew that this lady was my birth mother and I knew a little about my brothers and sisters. By this time, my mom had already given birth to another child who was just one year younger than me. I remembered little about my mom's side of the family because prior to this mishap, my mom made only one visit to see me in LaGrange and I traveled to Atlanta a few times with my father.

That morning, and every morning afterwards, I woke up depressed and lonely. I wasn't in the mood to talk to anyone. I was like a zombie at the age of five. I cried each and every day wishing I would see my dad and step-mom again. I would sit on the bed looking out the window waiting for my dad and stepmom to appear in my view, but unfortunately they didn't. Days, weeks, and months went by without any sign of my parents, and I started to believe that I would never see them again.

Finally, I began to open up to my family. I didn't talk nor play with anyone during the first couple of weeks there. We lived in Barn Homes housing apartments and for anyone who knows about Barn Homes will tell you that it wasn't the safest place to rear your child. Once I began to play with my siblings, we walked to a church service that was held outside in our neighborhood. I really didn't understand who God was or what He did, but I enjoyed going to this church service. I don't think anyone understood or cared how I felt as a child, but I was hurting during my stay in Atlanta with my mom.

One day while playing outside with my older brother, I remember seeing this white two-door truck pull up in front of the apartment. As I looked to see who it was I noticed that it was my dad and stepmom getting out of the truck. I dropped everything and started running towards them. This had to be one of the best days in my life. My heart was filled with joy and I was excited. I knew I was finally going home to a place I missed and loved. I didn't even care if I told my mom or my siblings goodbye, but it wasn't because I didn't like them. Sometimes children really don't care too much about others feelings and that's how I felt. It was like they didn't matter to me and years later I realized they meant a lot more to me. My dad asked my mom for my belongings and we were headed back to LaGrange. While driving home, I was told my dad and stepmom were fighting in court so they could get full legal custody of me.

Psalms 37:3-9 KJV

Trust In the Lord, and do good; so shalt thou dwell in the land, and verify thou shalt be fed. Delight thyself also in the Lord: and he shall give thee the desires of thine heart. Commit thy way unto the Lord; trust also in him; and he shall bring it to pass. Rest in the Lord, and wait patiently for him: fret not thyself because of him who prospereth in this way, because of the man who bringeth wicked devices to pass.

The Accident

As time went on and as I grew older, I began to love my stepmom's family more and more. Her family embraced me as if I was their own and that was the greatest feeling in the world. I was in the first grade now and I began to make friends and enjoy my life in LaGrange. One of my closest friends lived across the street and all the kids in the neighborhood had at least one bicycle with no working brakes. Riding a bike wasn't the safest thing to do without brakes, but we learned how to stop the bike with one special tool, our feet. Yes, we would stop the bike with our feet and sometimes we were barefoot. Sounds crazy, huh? But it worked.

One evening my closest friend and I were playing outside and decided to take our bikes for a ride. We were being just like all the children in the neighborhood riding up and down the road. I never thought that riding a bike would change my life. Of course my bike didn't have brakes but I didn't care because I knew how to stop the bike with my "special tools." So as we were riding our bikes down the end of a windy road, there was a four way intersection. At that intersection was stop signs, and for some reason, on this day, I decided to ignore the stop signs. While riding down the road, I looked over to my friend to see how far away he was because we were racing to the finish line which was past the stop sign.

A minute after I looked at him, it was lights out for me. I woke up in the hospital in a state of confusion because the last thing I remember was looking over towards my friend. After waking up I remember seeing my family, and how surprised everyone was to see the condition I was in. When I came to my senses, I realized that I could only move one of my legs. My left leg was propped in a harness, hanging in the air above the bed with a pin through it. I didn't understand what was going on, so I started asking my family what happened.

My stepmother began to tell me the whole story. She said because I didn't stop at the stop sign, a car hit me. She was at the house cleaning and cooking when a friend of mine ran to her house to deliver the bad news. When she finally came to me, the paramedics, police officers and a huge crowd were all surrounding me. She had to break through them to get to me and she told me I was crying and in pain; but I don't remember any of it. Reports said the car knocked me a few feet in the air and when I landed, I broke one of the largest bones in my leg. I was rushed to the hospital to have surgery on my broken leg.

I was in the hospital for more than three months; and spent Christmas and New Year's in the hospital. My grandfather spent most of the nights with me while my parents went to work. My parents and other family members were also there to spend the night when they were off work. Lying in a hospital bed made for a long three months. I couldn't move my entire body nor could I get up to walk, and besides playing my video games, it was pretty boring. I was missing school and friends but surprisingly some friends came to visit me.

Once my leg began to heal, I was put into a body cast that covered me from the bottom of my neck down to my ankle. While in the body cast, the only thing I could do was lay in my bed for another three months. I watched my friends play outside from the window and some came to keep me company and play video games. Just as I did in the hospital, I had to use the restroom right there from my bed. It was very uncomfortable and embarrassing at times. Until I was able to go back to school, I received homebound education services.

After a couple of months, I was finally out of my body cast but there was one small problem: I still couldn't walk. My legs were too weak and I had to learn how to walk again. For a couple of weeks I was still on bed rest, however, one afternoon my cousin came over to play hide-and-seek from my bed. I decided to get up from my bed to try and stand for the first time in months. I got up holding onto the bed without help and decided to take it to another level, I started taking one step at a time until I was walking, but I had to hold on to something. Once my family found out, everyone was so excited and happy for me. I had to attend many physical therapy sessions so I could strengthen my legs and bend them again. Unfortunately, even today, I am not able to bend my left leg completely. From that day on, I was on crutches and headed back to school.

Oh No!

I was young but very mature for my age. From the time I was in the first grade to the fifth, I experienced a lot in my life that would make me into the man I am today. During this time, I would figure out that my dad and stepmom were using drugs.

I was in the third grade and my stepmom took me to school one morning. While we were riding I picked up her purse looking for change for lunch. I thought I gave her the small purse back; instead it was lying on top of my book bag. So I got out of the car just like any other day, told my stepmom goodbye and headed into school. While in class I received a call to the office, on the way I figured something was wrong. At the office I saw my stepmom standing in the hall way waiting for me. Once I reached her I realized she was looking for her purse. I told her that it should have been in the car, but she said she did not see it. So we went to the car to look for it and didn't see anything. I also went back to the classroom to check my book bag, but there was no sign of it. I could tell in her eyes that she was a little worried about her purse being missing. I was responsible for losing her purse and the rest of my day didn't go so well, because I hated it when I thought anyone was mad at me. Even though she didn't say it, I could tell she was upset.

She left the school and I went back to class. Once the school day was over, I received more bad news. I was told that a school official found my stepmom's purse on the side of the street where she dropped me off. Apparently, when I got out of the car that morning, the purse fell on the ground. Once school began, a school official saw it and picked up the purse. School officials opened the purse so they could identify the owner and came across more than they expected. In the the purse, they found my stepmom's driver's license, money, and a bag of marijuana. Because of the marijuana, the school reported it to the police, which resulted in her license being suspended and a fine.

The Friend

A year later when I was nine, a friend of the family came from Chicago to LaGrange to visit family and friends. He resided with us for most of this stay. I really didn't see him much because he was in and out of the house. However, I noticed my parents continued to use drugs with this friend.

Then came a night I would never forget. I was in my bed sleeping and all of a sudden I was awakened by a loud noise. From my bed, I could see the front door. When I opened my eyes, the front door flew open and in stormed the police. Officers were everywhere, too many to count. They went into my parents' room and put them in handcuffs. I was confused and scared. I didn't want my parents going to jail and didn't want to be taken to a group home or somewhere worse. I began to cry as I saw my parents in the handcuffs. As the police officers searched, they totally destroyed our house. At that point, I knew what they were looking for, drugs. I found out that the friend my parents allowed to live with us was selling drugs from our house. The police came to end the madness. While they were searching for drugs, I remember hearing one of the officers tell my parents that if they found any more empty bags of marijuana they would lock them up. Well praise God they didn't find any more empty bags of marijuana in our house. My parents were set free of the handcuffs and I was able to go back to bed, realizing that our house was in a wreck. That friend of my parents was never seen again.

Reflections

Discuss how do you turn loneliness or boredom into productive activity?

Chapter 3

The Dark

When I was around the age of ten and in the fifth grade, I started to see a cycle in my life. I remember when I was six years old our electricity was turned off. We had no lights, water, or even air conditioning or heat. One afternoon I got off the bus, went into my house and noticed that it was very quiet and no one was home. I knew then that the lights were off. I began to cry and cry and asked myself "Why does this keep happening to us?" I wondered how would I take a bath, how would we eat, and how would I be on time for school in the morning.

Later that night I was hungry and needed something to eat. The electricity was still off and I decided to go ask a family member if I could have something to eat. After walking to their house, they made me a plate of food. I went outside to eat my meal. While I was eating, I overheard a conversation that would also change me forever. I heard my family talk about me eating their food and something about my parents. My body began to swell with anger because I was just a child in need of a meal and they really didn't want to feed me. When I heard the conversation, I started crying and didn't want to eat food from their house any longer. From that day on I told myself that I would never ask anyone for food or anything again. I told myself that I would rather die than ask anyone for anything. I left my family member's house and cried while I walked home. I couldn't believe what I had just heard and for some reason I never told my parents.

After a year of having our electricity off, I became used to the fact of not having electricity in the house. Every time we moved into another house our electricity would be disconnected, leaving us in the dark. My stepmom would wake me up for school and would get dressed in the dark sometimes wearing unclean clothes. I was depressed and sad going to school. I always told myself that I wouldn't be living like that forever. I always knew that life, especially mine, could be better than this. I would go to school and act out to keep from crying. I was the class clown and I felt I had to be because I had SO much pressure and anger built up inside. I decided I had to go to school and make jokes about everything so I wouldn't think about my problems.

What's for Dinner?

While I was growing up I realized that we were poor. I honestly believe that my stepmom and dad would have had the money if it weren't for their drug use. My dad would take his check to buy drugs before he would pay the bills or bring home food.

Many days I would come home and find there was no food in the house and my parents were broke. After hearing my family members talk about me eating at their house, I wouldn't dare think about going and asking anyone for food. I would sit at home and cry until I couldn't cry any more because I was hungry. My parents didn't come to my room the way I wanted to let me know everything would be ok or they would find a way for me to eat. I would cry myself to sleep so I couldn't feel the pain of hunger. I would go to bed many nights hungry and pray to God that everything would get better.

Sometimes the only meal I would get would be in school breakfast and lunch. You better believe that I never wanted to miss a day of school because I knew I could at least have two meals for the day. Still, eating breakfast and lunch at school will not satisfy a child through the entire day, imagine how it felt. Just imagine your child only having the opportunity to eat during school.

The pain and anger of not having what I needed in life drove me to hang out with friends who weren't a good influence on me. I was too young to have a job, so I told myself that I would just take what I needed. I would go to the local grocery store and stuff things in my pocket and walk out of the store. While doing this, I believe that I had to be the most nervous person in the world. I was scared I would get caught and go to jail, making a bad name for myself. Stealing was something I never wanted to do; it was something I felt I had to do to survive. Sometimes I would steal candy and sell it to students in school so I could make a little money. Things were hard for me; but that's not a reason to take things that didn't belong to me. I'm not proud of what I did, but that's what I knew at the time. Even at a very young age, I was appreciative of any-and everything I got in life and the smallest things made me happy. It was so bad that I remember digging in the trash can at a Goodwill store, finding and looking for things my family and I could use. It was something that I never wish upon any child.

Remembering

By now, you may be wondering whether I ever heard from my birth mom again. If you remember, I told you that my granddad was dating my aunt. Well, that aunt had a son who always looked up to my granddad as a father figure. This guy was my cousin, Arthur. From the time I was six years old through ten years old, Arthur would come to LaGrange to pick me up and take me back to Atlanta to see the rest of my family. The first few times I didn't feel comfortable around my family in Atlanta but it was something I had to get used to. They were my family and I wanted to have a relationship with them. My mom had six children: three boys and three girls and I was the baby boy.

I remember that on one of my last trips to Atlanta I was hit with some very terrible news. My mom began to tell me the story of one of my older sisters. I tried to get a good picture of my sister in my head. I was so young I couldn't remember her and I only saw them maybe once a year. But sadly, I could not get a good mental picture; to be honest I really didn't remember who she was at this time. I was about ten years of age and my sister was thirty years old. My mom began to tell me that my sister spent the night over at a friend's house and the next day she noticed that my sister had not come home. My mom and siblings were worried and prayed for her safety. Weeks and weeks had passed after my mother reported my sister as a missing person. Police investigators found some teeth they thought may have belonged to my sister. They tested the teeth to my mom's DNA to see if it really was my sister. The results were a match. My mom told me they never found her body. After hearing these words, my heart dropped, I couldn't believe I had lost a sister this way. I always thought stuff like this happened to other people, not me and my family, but it was real. To this day it hurts to realize I lost a sister and I didn't really know her. The next day my cousin and I were headed back to LaGrange. I remember that being my last trip to Atlanta for a while. As time went on, I wouldn't hear from or see my birth mother or that side of my family for quite a while.

Reflections

Discuss things that happen that's beyond your control and what you should do about them.

_____
_____
_____
_____
_____
_____
_____
_____
_____
_____
_____
_____
_____
_____
_____
_____
_____
_____
_____

Discuss why it's important to try and control anger (James 1:19, be quick to listen and slow to speak and anger).

___

Discuss how acting out in school will not be in your best interest and the consequences of negative behavior.

___

Chapter 4

The Bucket

I was a 12 year-old sixth grade student at Callaway Middle School and just about everything in my life was going wrong. Instead of worrying about learning in school and getting my homework done, I was worrying about the bills. I wondered if my belongings would be on the side of the road when I got home from school. I worried so much because I saw the same events happen year after year after year. My life was a pattern. Every year our electricity got turned off and we had to move out of our house or we would find our furniture on the side of the road. I worried about it so much that school and other things in my life meant nothing. My mind was focused on how I would survive from day to day.

I always told myself that I was too young to worry about such things. But once again our lights were turned off and this time they were off for a long time. We had to eat, take baths, wash clothes and most of all, live in the dark. There were more nights without meals and no showers. I had too much pride to ask anyone, whether they were family members or not for help. I had to survive the best way I knew how. I cried just about every night, telling myself that life should be better than this and I would always ask God, "Why me? Why do I have to go through this all the time?"

We went so long without having running water in

the house that it became unbearable. I had to find some way to have fresh water. I noticed there was a white bucket in the house and I went to get it. I placed it on the front steps of the house and told myself I would wait. I waited on the rain. I waited until it rained so water could fill my bucket. This way I could have some water to wash clothes, clean the house and possibly drink it if I had to. Sometimes it didn't rain for a while and we had to go without, but what a happy day it was when it did rain.

I slept in the living room while I waited on the rain. I thought about this terrible life I had to deal with. I thought about me living in the dark with no electricity, no food, no friends and no nothing–just me living there. I thought about the time when that man touched me in a place where I didn't think he should have touched me. And I thought about the things he did to me–words cannot express how I felt. That wasn't right and it didn't feel right, it hurt and it was very uncomfortable. I asked myself why he raped me. What did I do to him? Why God, why me? I was just five years old. I thought about how I felt like my parents didn't love me and I told myself that no one else loved me, so why should I.

I felt life was getting too difficult for me and I couldn't take it anymore. No one knew how lonely I felt sitting in that dark living room with a knife in my hand thinking about taking my own life. I figured no one loved me, or would miss me. I thought about how my stepmom and I were in the dark with no food, lights, or clean clothes. I thought about the fact that my dad hadn't been home that entire week. Later on we learned that he was living in someone else's house with lights, food, water and everything I wished we had. Why would my father leave us in the dark with nothing while he was living in a house with electricity?

Many times I thought about taking sleeping pills to end my life. I thought, "Hey, this would be less painful than a knife." But it was God that wouldn't let me do it because He knew things wouldn't always be like this. I thank God I lived and didn't commit suicide.

Once it rained and my bucket was filled, I would take the bucket and wash my clothes. Since the washing machine could not work without electricity, I had to make something happen. I did the only thing that was left to do. I poured some water from my bucket in the tub; and as tears rolled down my face, I washed my clothes with a bar of soap. I would continue to tell myself that life would not always be like this forever and something had to change. I think what hurt me most was the fact I had to do it alone. Once I finished washing my clothes, I hung them somewhere in the house to dry for the next day. I woke up several mornings and found that my clothes weren't dry and I had to go to school wearing wet clothes. I took a jacket to sit on, so that people wouldn't notice that my clothes were wet or see a wet stain after I got up from sitting down. Many times people noticed my clothes were wet and made jokes. There were times in the winter when I had to stand out in the freezing cold wearing wet clothes but I never said a word to anyone.

I also used the bucket of water to wash myself instead of taking a bath before school. We used the water to do some house cleaning while it was still daylight outside. While in middle school, I tried alcohol and drugs to escape from the horrible life I was living. I never once enjoyed any of it and didn't want to continue this behavior. During this time, there was a breaking point in my life and I knew it had to get better. Circumstances were so bad that I decided to go live with Uncle Tony, my dad's brother. This change was a much better environment to live in but not long after I would move back home with my parents.

The Program

While living with my uncle, I became involved in an organization called Communities in School (CIS). I joined this organization when the site coordinator, Cindy McWhorter Bryant, heard from one of my teachers that I needed glasses. Mrs. Bryant contacted me and within two weeks I was wearing my first pair of glasses. I continued to stay involved with CIS because of their willingness to help students succeed and all of the first time opportunities I was experiencing. Just to list a few, I received a mentor, anger management assistance, health insurance, and dental care. I was honored with the CIS "Student of the Year Award," the "Optimist Award" from the Optimist Club, and a Young Life Scholarship. I was in the LaGrange Daily News for speaking on behalf of CIS to United Way and participated in my first Christmas parade. I also entered into a speaking contest and participated in leadership classes through CIS. The best part of it all was that it was free for me.

As you may have noticed, before joining CIS I didn't have many opportunities. CIS put positive role models in my life and gave me extraordinary opportunities. It was in this program that I learned I was somebody and my life meant something. Another incentive CIS provided was an after-school program, where we learned life skills, computer skills and a variety of life lessons. There were snacks provided (which I really enjoyed) and CIS provided transportation home for all the students. I remember my first time getting in the van to go home and meeting the van driver, Mr. Cofield. While I was experiencing wonderful things I never imagined, Mrs. Bryant was right there by my side. She took me to the eye doctor, the dentist and anywhere else I needed to go that year. She was so concerned and cared about me so much that she made sure I was well taken care of. I remember when I was heavily medicated after getting my wisdom tooth pulled and still in a light sleep, she picked me up and literally carried me to the car for the ride home. She went above and beyond for me. She was like another mother, the mother I thought every child should have. She will never know how much she means to me. I thank Mrs. Bryant for all she has done for me, even the things she did that no one knew about. I know in my heart that everything she did came from her heart. She also wanted the best for me even when it came down to my language and grammar. She would correct every word I said incorrectly and make me say it repeatedly until I got it right. She was a tough cookie, but I know now that she meant well by it and wanted me to succeed. To put the icing on the cake, I was invited to be in her wedding.

Reflections

Not sure why I didn't list anything but I'm sure you can come up with some discussion points.

Chapter 5

Born Again

It was 2002 and I was thirteen years old. After a couple of weeks of riding in the van with Mr. Cofield, he invited everyone to church. At the same time, I was also praying to God to help me and make things better for my family.

The following Sunday I was on the van headed to church. Once I saw the pastor of the church he looked familiar. Once I got a closer look and noticed the other church members, I remembered their faces. Many years before, my aunt was a member of this church and I would attend with her and her children. I felt at home. I really enjoyed myself at church and knew I had to come back. After church was over we headed back home. Every time I saw Mr. Cofield I would ask him something about Jesus. Oh, I had a lot of questions! Who is He? How does He work? How can a person get saved? It was like I was thirsty to hear more about God and I could tell Mr. Cofield didn't mind explaining it to me.

The next Sunday I was back in church. I had hoped my family would come with me but they didn't. I had recognized a void in my life, and the missing link was God. It was during that service I walked down the aisle to give my life to Christ. Once I received Jesus as my Lord and Savior I felt something that I never felt before.

It is amazing how God will choose you out of your entire family to serve Him. As a young child, I thought parents were supposed to become Christians before their children, but not in my case. God will choose the ones who will be faithful, and willing to serve Him. He will also raise up that individual so they can be a light to their family and cause the family to draw near to God.

After giving my life to Christ and sharing the good news with everyone I came in contact with, people started to hold me to a very high standard. What do I mean by this? I couldn't do anything without someone asking me if that was Christ-like. I had to explain to them it was ok to joke around and laugh or it was ok to listen to music other than gospel music. However, they did not want to hear that. I believe some people wanted me to walk around wearing a suit on holding my Bible. If I did that they would still find something else to point out. I told myself I knew right from wrong and I was going to be me and live my life and if the critics didn't like it, oh well. At that point is when I learned to be myself and strive to be the best I could be.

2 Corinthians 5:17 KJV

"Therefore if any man be in Christ, he is a new creature: old things are passed away; behold, all things are become new."

Do you remember when you first received Jesus Christ into your heart and felt a way that nobody else could make you feel? Well, that's how I felt and I just had to tell people. I went home telling my family about Jesus and how good He is. In the eighth grade, I went to school telling everybody about this man named Jesus.

Within a month's time I became a member of the church. Every Sunday I had to request the van because I asked all of my friends to come to church with me. I walked in church with close to ten friends every Sunday because I wanted people to experience Jesus the way I had. I knew if they did, they would feel great. The Bible helps us to understand we are the salt of the earth and if the salt has lost its savor, wherewith shall it be salted? We are also the light of the world and should let our light shine before men. (Matthew 5:13- 16) I will add that it is so easy to lose our savior and lose our focus of the goal of winning souls for Jesus because we get so caught up in our own lives.

Mark 16:15 NIV

"He said to them, Go into all the world and preach the gospel to all creation."

The Phone Call

Before my eighth grade year ended, I moved back home with my parents from my uncle's house. Uncle Tony was a very stern man and because my parents were so laid back and didn't say much to me, I didn't like the rules my uncle had for his house. My parents would somewhat let me do whatever I wanted to do but my uncle wasn't having it. I am very grateful my uncle allowed me to stay with him because we had food on the table, running water and lights in the house. In other words, I was being taken care of and felt like my uncle really cared. He also pushed my education and became involved in what I was doing. I just didn't like following the rules because up until then I had none.

While living with my uncle and going to church with the Cofield's, they took me places outside of church. I also used to call Mr. Cofield to ask for Godly advice. During this time I met the Duckett Family, and spent many weekends at their home as well. The Ducketts knew I didn't have the best life. This family played a special part in my life and will never know how much they mean to me.

After living with my uncle for a couple of months, I moved back home and started to attend a summer program with Communities In Schools. Mr. Cofield was having some health issues, so he didn't drive the van much that summer. The van driver took everyone home and dropped them off at their house, except for me. I used to be so ashamed of how my house looked and didn't want the students on the bus picking on me. The reason I was so concerned about their opinions was because I picked on everyone else. I would make jokes and laugh at someone else's house if it didn't look nice.

I would tell the bus driver to drop me off at the top of the street and walked to a house everyday that wasn't mine. One day after getting off the van and walking to my house, I stepped on the porch and instantly knew the lights were off. I was so used to the lights being turned off that it no longer surprised me. As I walked into the house, there was no one to be found. I sat on the couch and began to cry. I thought things like this shouldn't happen to Christian people.

I began to ask God, "Why is this happening to me again?" I told Him I was trying to live right and do things according to His will. I cried so hard that I started to get a headache. Later, I called Mrs. Bryant, the Ducketts, and the Cofields and explained what was going on in my life. I always told myself I would never ask for help, but there was something about these people that was so genuine. I knew I could count on them. I called the Ducketts and the Cofields to ask if I could spend one night with them. It was late in the evening and they suggested that I go down to my grandmother's house and stay the night and they would come to get me tomorrow. I told them I would, but I stayed in the house and cried myself to sleep. After I got home from camp, the Ducketts and Cofields pulled up in front of my house.

Mrs. Duckett was the executive director of Communities In Schools of Troup County when I started the program and the Ducketts were members of my church. While I spent a lot of time with the Cofields, I also spent time with the Ducketts. They would come pick me up from my house and allow me to spend time in each of their homes. The Ducketts have been a blessing to me more than others may know. They taught me values, blessed me with clothes and also allowed me to experience a warm, lovely home. They also taught me about eating more healthy. Anyone who knows the Ducketts knows they eat healthy. I remember when I first started to spend time with the Ducketts, I would carry a small grocery bag filled with clothes. They gave me a black duffel bag and told me to use it whenever I went somewhere. I really didn't understand why the black bag was important. As I grew older I understood that the Ducketts were trying to get me to think on a higher level.

I was so excited to see that others really cared and always asked myself, "Why are these people being so nice to me?" The feeling was so unreal. The time came when I decided to go spend the night with the Cofields, not because I didn't like the Ducketts or because the Cofields were better people. I decided to go with the Coficlds because they had two sons that were a little closer to my age and we were becoming friends. With the Cofield family, I knew I would have someone to relate who was near my age. I really do appreciate all that the Ducketts did for me. They have been a blessing to me in more ways than they will ever know. I am grateful for both families and for Mrs. Bryant. All were willing to help me in any way I needed. After letting my parents know what I was going to do, I jumped in the car and we drove off.

Psalms 50:15 KJV

And call upon me in the day of trouble: I will deliver thee, and shalt glorify me."

Reflections

Why is following house rules important when you aren't in charge or paying bills?

Chapter 6

The Cofields

When I arrived at the Cofield's house, I said to myself that I had hit the jackpot. I also thought the Cofields were rich and I knew I would like it there.

When I got out of the car the only belongings I had were a grocery sack full of clothes, the clothes I had on, and the shoes on my feet. Regardless of how many clothes I had, I was still happy spending the night with the Cofields and having a nice place to lay my head. It didn't take much to please me.

Later that night I had my first dinner with the Cofields. We had steak, baked potato, and salad. After seeing and eating this meal with a smile on my face, I knew that I made it. In the Cofield's and Duckett's home, we ate as a family at the table. This was something I had rarely experienced and I enjoyed every moment of it.

I realized this was where I wanted to live and going back home wasn't an option. After a couple of days, I talked to Mrs. Cofield about me staying with them for more nights. Mrs. Cofield was always the first person any of her children would talk. She is very laid back and easier to talk to than Mr. Cofield. There was just something about him and don't worry, he knows it.

Mrs. Cofield is like most mothers, caring, loving

and made sure that everyone in the house was taken care of, not only physically but emotionally as well. Mr. Cofield, on the other hand, is a very stern and strict father for all of the right reasons. It was like going into a job interview everytime Maurice, Quize or I wanted to talk to him. We had to have everything planned out and be prepared to answer questions. If you didn't, then you can forget about going or doing anything. He didn't know that we gave him the nickname "the investigator." Years later I would understand why Mr. Cofield did the things he did and I catch myself doing the same things.

After talking to Mrs. Cofield, she expressed that she would love for me to stay as long as I wanted. According to their testimony, they allowed multiple people and families to live with them, so me asking to stay longer wasn't a problem.

She told me to go ask Mr. Cofield so he could give it an ok or not, and that had to be the most nervous moment I ever witnessed. Not because he was mean or anything but I was afraid of him saying no, for whatever reason, and I couldn't take any more rejections in my life. But I finally got enough courage to ask him and to my surprise he said, "Yes." He didn't have to think about it or get back with me later. He told me yes right there on the spot. I was excited, but I didn't let them see too much of it.

When I first came over to the Cofield's, I slept in their younger son's room. There were no extra beds in the house so Quize allowed me to rest in his bed while he slept with his older brother Maurice or on the couch. One afternoon, Mr. Cofield and the boys were riding through town and we noticed a twin size bed at this yard sale. As we looked at the bed, we noticed it was identical to the beds the Cofields had at home. We were amazed to see what we found and knew it had to be God who led us to this yard sale.

When it was time to purchase the bed, Mr. Cofield didn't turn around and ask me if I had the money or if I knew a way to help pay for it. I wanted to feel good about the purchase of the new bed, but a little part of me didn't. It was so hard for me to accept gifts or allow people to be a blessing to me. For once in my life, I felt love and to know people really cared for me was a great feeling.

Two years after I went to live with the Cofields, a guy name Ansu Kenneth moved in with us. Living in a three bedroom house meant Quize once again had to give up his bed so Ansu would have a place to lay his head. Maurice and Quize slept in the same bed for a year so that Ansu and I could have a place to sleep. I don't know any other young guys that would have done that and not complain about it.

Throughout my years living with the Cofields, we had some good days and–just like in any other household–we had some bad days. But I will say that Mr. and Mrs. Cofield treated all of us as if we were their own. If one got in trouble, we all got in trouble. If one got praised, we all got praised.

Within the household we all had chores and rules to abide by. Looking back, sometimes I can see that Mr. and Mrs. Cofield tried to teach us to look out for one another although we weren't blood brothers. If one of us didn't wash dishes or clean up the living room, before the next morning, everyone would be punished for it. They would take all of our cell phones and for days, sometimes weeks at a time for not following the rules. I remember one day when I expressed to Mr. Cofield I was too old for them to take my cell phone. He told me that as long as I was living under his roof I would follow his rules and would continue to take my phone whenever he wanted to. Oh! I became more angry than I already was and thought this man had to be the meanest person alive. I wanted my phone and didn't want to hear about rules.

One thing I learned about Mr. Cofield is that he always tried to teach us a lesson; even if we didn't understand it. Mrs. Cofield didn't play either. Even though she never wanted us to get in trouble, when the house didn't get cleaned she would wake all of us up at three o'clock in the morning to clean. Every day wasn't bright and sunny, but the fun and exciting days definitely outweighed the bad ones. I would never take back my experience with the Cofields.

Looking back, Mr. and Mrs. Cofield were right. In just about everything they did, they were teaching us how to become good husbands and fathers one day. There are so many stories I can tell you about living with them. I could probably write a book just about my time in their home! If you ever invite me to speak at your church, school, or business function, we can talk all day about it.

Maurice and Quize also gave up a lot for Ansu and me. I never heard Maurice or Quize tell us they were ready for us to leave. Nor did I ever hear them say anything like that amongst themselves. It was a blessing and it felt great to know I was finally accepted into a family where no one talked about you. We always kept each other laughing, doing this brought us closer together. They really made me feel comfortable living with them and we all grew up knowing we were a real family. I love each and every one of them as my own blood family.

Like I stated earlier, Mrs. Cofield took care of everyone in their home. She acted just like any mother would towards her children and she really did treat Ansu and me like her own. She was a very strong woman during times when Mr. Cofield was sick. Even when she was sick herself, she still worked and made a way for us. They never once told me or Ansu that we had to leave and every time I think of this I get emotional because they could have. They all loved us so much. I knew this was my family and I wasn't going anywhere. All of the boys would help out any way we could; cleaning up the house, cooking or bringing food home after work, or cutting the grass.

The entire time I was at the Cofield's house my parents didn't come over once to check up on me, see how I was doing, make sure I was still alive, or to offer the Cofields money or any kind of support for taking care of me. Not one time did the Cofields ask my parents for money or receive government assistance for me. It was the blessings of God that kept everything together. Although we never talked about it, I truly believe my parents wanted me to come back home, but I didn't want to because I was afraid of the electricity getting turned off again. I talked to and visited my family often. Mr. & Mrs. Cofield made sure I kept in touch with my natural family. I asked to spend one night with the Cofields, which then turned into six years. It was in those six years that I would learn more about myself and my relationship with Christ. I am thankful for all the late night and early morning conversations with Mr. and Mrs. Cofield. Those times of receiving wisdom and understanding will always be with me.

Reunion

After being in church and learning more about God and forgiveness, I began to think about my mom and the rest of the family back in Atlanta. It had been about five years since I heard or saw any of them. I was hurt because I couldn't believe that my own mother didn't try to come see me, call me, or do anything to reach me. In spite of that, I wanted to forgive.

I was nearly fifteen years old when I asked my granddad and Uncle Tony to help me find my family. By this time my granddad and my aunt were no longer dating and had lost contact with each other. One afternoon after I got out of school, the three of us headed to Atlanta on a quest to find my family.

None of us knew where we were going. We were just going to ride through the old neighborhood my granddad was familiar with. After riding in the back seat of my uncle's green Ford Explorer, we finally reached a familiar face. My granddad found this lady he once knew and asked if she knew where we could find my mom or aunt. The lady didn't have a clue where my mom or aunt had moved. It was hard for anyone to keep up because they were always moving. We continued our quest until we saw a homeless guy my granddad knew. He asked him about my mom or aunt and thankfully, he knew something.

He didn't know exactly where my mom or aunt lived, but he knew what neighborhood my aunt lived in and gave us directions. It was getting dark and we were still riding around trying to figure out the right house and street for my aunt. I was giving up hope, telling myself that we would never find them like this. Then we spotted a man walking down the streets of Atlanta. We asked him if he knew of my aunt and he said she lived two houses down from where we were. I suddenly became scared and excited at the same time. Why? Because I knew this was the day I had waited for. I was about to see my family.

We got out of the car and knocked on the door. My mother's oldest brother came to the door. Once he noticed it was my granddad and uncle, he was excited. My aunt was so happy to see my granddad and me that she was in shock; she couldn't understand how we found her at that time of night. She called my mother to share that I was at her house. About thirty minutes later, I saw my mom, younger sister and older brother walk through the door. My mom was so excited; I was about ten years older since we had last seen or talked to each other.

We talked for what seemed like forever, but we had to leave because I had school the next morning. Before we left, my mom and I exchanged phone numbers. From that moment on, I have gotten to know my mom and siblings better. We talk often and I visit as much as I can.

After the visit, I felt I finally had closure. I was excited to start on a clean slate with my family. The more I was around them, the more I couldn't believe these people were my biological family. So many of my siblings and mom have so much in common and I was happy to witness it all.

At Church

I felt complete. I was a young Christian man in a loving family. Deep down inside I knew that my dad, mom, and stepmom loved me even if they didn't show it the way I thought they should. They raised me the best way they could and I love them so much.

I was a leader in my church and I walked around preaching to everybody I came in contact with; sometimes we would even shout. There were so many times when I couldn't wait to get to church because I knew I would hear something that was going to change my life. Later on I started sharing the word of God to a class of middle school students. I was very involved in my church and my passion for people, especially the youth, grew more and more. In high school, friends and family were giving me nicknames like pastor, preacher man, reverend, or even preacher boy.

There is one nickname stay with me to this very day. At Destiny Worship International Church, where I am a member, Mrs. Maria Ransom, who is like a mother to me, started calling me Bishop. She was the only one who called me that for years. Somehow the name stuck with me and followed me to college and to this present day.

Reflections

Discuss why having responsibility for household chores is important and how unselfish behavior can benefit others.

Chapter 7

Graduating from High School

Graduating from high school was a dream come true. Few, and I mean very few, family members graduated, but I knew I had to. I came very close to not graduating. Before I could graduate I had to pass all five sections of the Georgia High School Graduation Test (GHSGT): writing, math, science, social studies and language arts. With my first attempt, I passed all of the sections except science and social studies. I had to retake both parts to graduate from high school. I took the science two more times until I passed. My final attempt to pass social studies was the last test offered before graduation. I'm sure you can imagine the pressure, stress, and amount of weight on my shoulders. I was prayed up like never before and ready to take the test and pass it so I could walk across that stage at graduation. Months had passed and it was a week before graduation. As time marched on, I became more nervous, too nervous to invite people to come to graduation. While sitting in class, I was called to the office and I knew it was time to find out my news. I slowly and nervously opened the letter, knowing that so much was at stake. The letter had one word–PASSED–and I fell to the floor with joy in my heart, thanking God Almighty for giving me the courage and confidence to take and pass the test. For a year I was worried about passing the GHSGT, but God had already figured it out.

In May of 2006, I was walking across the stage as a high school graduate. This meant a lot to me because I had a lot of family members on both sides of the family that never graduated. This was an important day for my family and me. Everyone was so excited and proud of me. My mom came from Atlanta, he Cofields, my dad, step- mom, and grandma were there as well. I even had members of my church family to support me. I remember the Ransom family made a big sign that read "Congratulations Fredrick." I felt so loved that day.

After high school, I attended West Georgia Technical College in LaGrange, Georgia where my major was business management. I went there to raise my grade point average (GPA) so I could attend another school with the Hope Scholarship. The Hope Scholarship is awarded to students who live in Georgia and attend state universities and colleges with a 3.0 or higher GPA in core classes.

While taking night classes, I worked two jobs. One was with Communities In Schools, the same organization that made such an impact in my own life. I was a mentor/tutor and traveled to four different elementary schools helping children with their academics. I also went worked for Kroger grocery store and Radio Shack. In the process, I was able to buy my first car for $500. Now you may think the car I bought wasn't any good for $500, but I can ensure you there were no major problems. It had a small oil leak and needed a minor paint job, but I wasn't worried about a paint job. I was just excited to finally have my first car.

After a year had passed, I was ready to transfer to Gordon College. A week before school started I called the school to make sure my financial aid would cover my tuition and housing. A young lady told me that I qualified for the Hope Scholarship. I knew that nothing from West Georgia Technical College transferred, but with that being said I was eligible for the Hope Scholarship because of my grades in high school. So yes, I graduated high school with a 3.0 GPA and didn't even know it.

Gordon College

I was finally moving out of the house and knew I could do anything I wanted to now. I could stay out as late as I wanted and there would be no curfew. In my mind, I knew I would have a lot of fun, but fun that I knew God would look at as sin. I was determined to graduate from Gordon College and make good grades. I was going to be the first in my immediate family to have a college degree and I could not let my family down. There were high hopes for me to finish college and I could not let myself down.

My first year at Gordon I lived in a residential dorm called Common C and in that dorm I met a few friends who I could laugh with and just be myself. On one particular night I asked my friends if they wanted to play "church" and they said, "Sure, why not." So I gave everyone a role such as Mary, the mother of Jesus, someone played the role of Peter, someone was the usher and of course I was the "Bishop." I would preach and preach while everyone else would shout and such. It was such a good time and that's how the name Bishop stayed with me. I didn't take the name lightly because after a few people started calling me Bishop, it soon covered the entire campus. It was so serious that many people thought Bishop was my birth name. Of course there were the people who didn't call me Bishop because they thought that if I wasn't a real Bishop there was no need to call me that. I didn't care if they called me Bishop or not, just as long as they called me Fredrick and not Fred. I also noticed that people started to look up to me and because of that I really had to watch what I said and did. To some people, I was the only representation of God in their lives.

God really blessed me at Gordon College and showed me favor with the faculty and staff. I will never forget the end of my first semester when the on-campus students had to move back home for the Christmas break. Right before school was out, I applied for a Resident Assistant (RA) position on campus. With that position, a student could work and be compensated by having their rent paid. My rent was $500 a month, all-inclusive with phone, cable, and utilities. So, having this position was something I needed. My dad was paying my rent, but every month I feared that he wouldn't come through with the payments. After applying for the job, I got an email from the Residence Life Office saying that I would be placed on the alternate list. If someone didn't want their position for whatever reason, I would be next in line.

After a while, I figured that I wouldn't get the position because school was going to start in about a week. About three days before school started I got a call from Ms. Shalanna Bank. She was my resident director in Commons C. Was it strange that the position was open in her building? I think not. She asked if I was still interested in the RA position and I told her without a doubt I was very much interested and asked when I could start. She asked if I could return to Gordon the next day and I told her I would be at Gordon in two hours. I was so excited that I was ready to start the job immediately. I thank God for her, the housing director, Ms. Tonya Coleman, and assistant director, Ms. Gratasha Banks, for all agreeing to hire me. It's not really strange that that door opened for me; it was all God's doing. When you trust in the Lord and live according to His will, He will reward you.

The next year I was voted president of the Student Government Association (SGA). I was excited but knew I had my work cut out for me. I still had my RA position while taking five classes. Because of the knowledge and wisdom God had given to me, I was able to lead the student body and maintain good grades. If it wasn't for the Cofields who always gave me little nuggets of wisdom, I probably would have given up. Thankfully, I was on top of things and I was commended for my good work.

Many people have gifts and talents to sing, dance, write, or play an instrument, but my gift was being a leader. It took me a long time to figure that out. I would always wonder why I couldn't sing, dance, or play an instrument and I was jealous of those that could. It took me years to finally find out who I was and what I could bring to the table. My maturity and communication skills were the gifts I needed to use.

During the time I was at Gordon College, God continued to show me favor with the president, vice president, faculty and staff members. Things that others couldn't do, God graced me with the ability to do. He also showed me favor with people off campus; the Banks, Haygoods, Hamms, and countless others were such blessings to me and treated me like one of their own.

Another year had passed and I decided not to participate in SGA any more. My decision was made only because I was approaching my last year and wanted to focus on my studies. A month into the semester there was a new organization at Gordon College called the Student African American Brotherhood (SAAB) and I was approached to join. After long deliberation I decided to do it. I knew this organization would bring about change among the African American males on the Gordon campus. After attending one meeting, I was voted president.

As I look back over the years, I realized that people were watching me no matter what I was doing, even when I thought they weren't. That's why I always told my peers to be careful what you do and say because someone is always watching you. In college, I learned more about myself, people, and friendship.

When my stepmom's mother, my grandmother, who I was very close to, passed away in May of 2009 I was truly heartbroken. Even though she wasn't my biological grandmother, she was the only grandmother I knew. I didn't know how I would get through this stage in my life because she meant so much to me. During the hard times of dealing with my grandma's death and trying to be strong for my stepmom and other relatives, I couldn't have handled any of that without my best friend, Chad Walker. He was there with me through it all and didn't complain one time. When I needed a shoulder, he was there and God used him to help me through the hard times. There were many hard times when Chad was there for me. I really appreciate him for being that kind of friend.

One nugget I'd like to leave with you is to be careful who you call your friend and who you allow in your inner circle. Those so-called "friends" will ride the journey with you for a moment but when trouble hits, they may abandon you. Now I'm not saying that everybody you meet will do this, but be very careful. I promise you will save yourself a lot of heartaches if you listen to this advice.

Many people, including family and friends, didn't know that I was in learning-support (remedial) classes when I first arrived at Gordon College. To exit out of them, I had to pass the Compass test for each of the three learning-support classes. While I passed two out of three, I twice failed the writing class, which made me a little depressed. I remembered that everything happens for a reason and it was all in God's plan. I just had to work harder the next time.

One of the reasons I struggled so badly was that in my early school years I absolutely hated reading. When other students would read or check out books from the library it made me envious of them. I picked on them because they were good readers and I wasn't. If a teacher called on me to read aloud in class, I got so nervous that I stumbled over words. Students would sometimes giggle to themselves which didn't make reading better for me.

I realized the real problem wasn't that I didn't like reading; the problem was that I didn't know how to read well. I went through school and life avoiding books, tools that are full of knowledge and wisdom. It wasn't until I was in college that I had to pay the price for not reading in my earlier years of life. Writing and reading go hand and hand and I had difficulty with both.

I also had to pass the Georgia Assessments for the Certification of Educators (GACE) test in order to be accepted in the education program in the State of Georgia. Some faculty and staff members at Gordon knew of my struggles and encouraged me and helped any way they could. I was encouraged to read more and stay committed to it. Well, I did just that. I started reading books and turned off one of the biggest distractions, the television, while I read. I got into the habit of not just reading but having a positive attitude about reading. When it came time to take the test, I knew I was going to pass the GACE and I did. I didn't stop there, I continued to read more and watch less television.

I encourage everybody to pick up a book, a magazine, or something that interests you and read it. Reading will open up a whole new world for you. Don't pay the cost for not reading and writing like I did. But it's amazing how a little boy who didn't like to read or know how to read well is writing his own book. What was meant to defeat me God used for my good. You can do the same. Whatever is defeating you, ask God to turn it around let it work for your good. I promise you it can happen.

Prior to graduation, I had to pass the reading portion of the Regent's Test. In the State of Georgia, the Board of Regents for the University System of Georgia ask that students enrolled in an undergraduate degree program pass the Regents' Reading Skills and the Regents' Writing Skills course as a requirement for graduation. After my fourth and fifth failures, I started to feel hopeless.

I graduated from Gordon College May 15, 2010, but only a few people knew that I didn't actually receive my degree that day. I didn't pass the Regent's test even after I was allowed to take it over and over again. I was too ashamed and embarrassed to tell anyone that I didn't pass it because I feared what they would think about me. I was able to participate in graduation and held my head high. The plan was for me to take the Regent's Reading Test the following summer and once I passed I would get my degree. Because of God's grace, I was able to walk across that stage. It was important for me to walk across the stage. If I didn't, I would have to wait another year to walk. Who wants to do that once they have already left the school?

I was excited at graduation because I knew I was going to be the first in my immediate family to have a college degree, even though it was an associate degree. During graduation I was missing two of the most important people in my life, my mom and dad. Was I hurt? Yes, because I could not understand why they weren't there. I was the only child either one of them had that graduated from college. I ignored both of them because I felt there were no excuses for them to miss my big day. I was mad, upset, but most of all I was hurt. I thought about my other family members who came. My stepmom, sister and the Cofields were all there to support me. At that point, that was all that really mattered. I always struggled with knowing if people really loved me or not. When I see my loved ones go out of their way for me it really brings me unexplainable joy. All of my family from Gordon College was there to celebrate this day with me and what a great day it was. I proudly walked across that stage. Even though I was hurt, I forgave my parents and told them that they better be there the next time I graduated.

I received an email on that following Monday stating that Gordon College had been completely exempted from the Regents testing. So what did that mean for me? It meant that walking across that stage was not in vain because I was finally a graduate of Gordon College. You see how God works?

When I graduated from Gordon, I knew I had given it all I had to give. I did just about everything at Gordon and I thank God for allowing me to do so. I went through a lot and learned a lot there. The school and people there will always hold a special place in my heart. The faculty and staff made my experience at Gordon a great one.

Reflections

Discuss perseverance, particularly if something doesn't work out initially.

Discuss advantages of having someone to talk to, especially during difficult times.

_____
_____
_____
_____
_____
_____
_____
_____
_____
_____

Discuss why knowing how to read is important. Discuss ways you can improve reading skills.

_____
_____
_____
_____
_____
_____
_____
_____
_____

Chapter 8

Statistics

Statistics are used to categorize all types of people: rich and poor, black and white, male and female.

If you strictly go by the statistics, you could say that I'm supposed to be or have been in prison or that I'm supposed to have children out of wedlock. Statistics would lead you to believe that I'm supposed to be on drugs or at least selling drugs or that I'm supposed to be wearing my pants below my waist and that I'm not supposed to be in college. Statistics don't tell the whole story. The devil himself has tried to make me become a statistic and people have said I would be nothing in life. Even though I lived in the dark, didn't have food to eat, lived in the projects, tried drugs and alcohol, and took things that weren't mine, it's by the grace and mercy of God I still am not a statistic. Don't let your past define who you are today.

If I had not been rescued and moved in with the Cofield's, I probably would have become a statistic. Many of the guys I called friends have fallen into the statistic category. When I think of the goodness of Jesus and all that He brought me from, I just can't help but tell Him "Thank You." I'm not supposed to be here today. I was supposed to be dead a long time ago, but I'm here. When I look back, I learn that the devil had to take his hands off me. When he did, he couldn't stop me any more.

I can't say enough about the grace of God. I have no children out of wedlock because I'm waiting for marriage. I am not on any type of drugs, nor have I ever sold any. I wear my pants around my waist and most of the time with my shirt tucked in. I have received one degree and I'm working on another. I'm a man of God who strives each and every day to be more like Jesus. I'm not perfect, I have made many mistakes in my life and all of my decisions haven't been good ones. I'm here today to let you know that I'm still human and that because of God's grace and mercy, I am able to ask for forgiveness and move on with my life.

Mrs. Cofield would always say to me, "Don't let your past determine who you are today because the past is just that–the past." Don't let the devil or anyone place a calling on your life. Open up the Bible and read God's Word to tell you who you are and what you can do as a child of God. You know you make the devil mad when you are not listening to him, so DON'T! This is one more reason to praise God, because we don't have to be what people or the devil say we are. I have overcome the odds and so can you.

Have you ever been on a roller coaster ride? If so, you can remember that on a roller coaster you have your up-and-down moments. You sometimes go left and then right. For most of us, when it's over you're glad it's over. My life has been a lot like a roller coaster ride. I have had my high points, I've had many low points, I've taken right turns and left turns. But that's part of life, you know? Everybody has felt like they have been on a roller coaster ride in life. But guess what? We made it and we are still here. I'm here to inform readers that it doesn't matter what it may look or feel like. God has the final answer and he will bring you out of your storm. Just continue to wait on the sunshine. One good thing about a storm is that it only lasts for so long. When it passes, the sun comes out and it's a brighter day.

I always tell people not to feel sorry for me because I know why I had to go through what I went through. For many years I wished that I was part of another family that was a "together family." I realized that I am who I am today because of what I have been through!

If I could go back in time, I wouldn't change anything about my past. I believe that everything happens for a reason and I went through all the hurts, pains, feelings of rejection, and struggles for a reason. I would be envious of other families and other people. I realized they were always missing one thing; Jesus Christ. With Him I have everything; without Him I would have nothing. I'm not perfect and there are things I need to work on. That's why I thank God for His Glory each and every day. My past made me the man I am today! So for those of you out there, don't feel bad about what you went through. Realize that you had to go through it. It was hard and you wanted to give up, but didn't. You should thank God that you didn't give up. See the things we go through aren't really just for us but it is for someone else. Someone else is going through the same thing that you have faced in your life and because of that God can use you as a living testimony. Just think about all of the people your story can touch and minister to. Even though I had to grow up fast and poor, I thank God that I wasn't born in a rich family because I wouldn't be the person I am today. I know that most children say, "I wish my parents were rich." I understand that, but I don't take anything for granted and the smallest thing brings me joy.

2 Thessalonians 3:3 (KJV)

"For the Lord is faithful, who shall establish you, and keep you from evil."

Our Young People

One of the most important things I like to do is encourage and motivate young people around the world.

Youth face a lot in their lives, even at a young age. Hearing a testimony from someone that has been there and has come out on top could be very inspirational to them. The most important thing I tell them is to serve God and put Him first because nothing in this world is worth not having Jesus in your life. Family and friends may turn their backs on you, but there is one person who will never leave you nor forsake you and that person is Jesus Christ.

I always encourage our young people to not just attend church and sit there while the service is going on. There are things we all need from God and we cannot afford just to sit there in church and let God's blessing pass us by. I'm not saying you have to shout and jump around, but be engaged and listen to what the pastor is saying. It will change your life forever. Parents, encourage your children to bring their bibles to church. Mr. Cofield would always tell us that the bible is like a weapon, you may never know when you need to use it but at least be prepared. It's like a police officer, he or she carries their gun (weapon) with them wherever they may go. There are times when they won't use it but if something happens, at least they are prepared. It's the same with the bible; if the enemy attacks you will be prepared because you have the word (bible) with you. Flip through the pages and you defeat the devil with the Word of God.

After leaving my home church to attend college, I thought I would find another church just like home. I visited a couple of churches nearby while I was at Gordon College, but t most of them didn't feed me in the same way spiritually.

A person going to college will have so much freedom trouble they can get into. I don't want you to think I went to Gordon College and went completely wild. But if a person isn't careful, he or she can. That's why I was looking for a church to attend, to keep me grounded. Now, did I mess up while I was at Gordon? Yes, I sure did. When I look back, there are some things I can't believe I've done. One thing is for sure, I have learned from my mistakes and repented for the things I've done that weren't in the will of God.

For years I was off track with God's will. There was a void in my life that needed to be filled. I tried to fill it with people, doing things I know that were wrong, work and school, but none of that worked. Years later I realized that my life was empty and I got tired of putting on a mask and not being genuine in my relationship with Christ. I returned to my home church and started getting my relationship with Christ back on the right track.

We are all going to sin, that is a fact. God will forgive us over and over again, but don't let sin and guilt keep you staying away from God.

Matthew 18:21-22

"Then Peter came to Jesus and asked, "Lord, how many times shall I forgive my brother or sister who sins against me? Up to seven times?"

"Jesus answered, "I tell you, not seven times, but seventy-seven times."

John 15:7 KJV

"If ye abide in me, and my words abide in you, ye shall ask what ye will, and it shall be done unto you."

What's in Your Bucket?

People will experience different struggles, trials and tribulations, but it's up to the individual to determine what the outcome will be. We can let our situations defeat us or we can come out on top of our situations victoriously.

So the question is, what is in your bucket? My bucket not only contained rainwater, but was filled with hurt, pain, worry and molestation. I didn't let that defeat me instead I used it all to become a young, successful man who's after God's heart. Every decision I made has not been one God would approve of, but I can only ask God to continue to show me His grace and mercy so that I can make better decisions.

If your bucket is filled with rejection from when your dad left home and you never heard from him again, or from when a person touched you in a way that you knew wasn't right, you can empty that bucket. Your bucket may be filled with depression, envy, worry, or financial issues; empty all of that from your bucket. Refill your bucket with joy, peace, love, faith, money, hope and other good things. Don't let your past determine who you are or can be today. God wants you to be the best person you can be, so don't let your pity party last too long. Make the best out of your situation. Make your problems work for you and not against you.

1 Peter 5:7 KJV

"Casting all your care upon him; for He careth for you"

Reflections

Discuss what goals you can set when statistics and seemingly the world is against you.

Discuss how you handle self-doubt.

Chapter 9
What I'm Up to Now

This is my first book, published at age 24 and my plan doesn't stop at this book. My prayer is that many will follow. I graduated from Gordon College, but I wasn't going to stop there. I enrolled in the Early Childhood Education program at the University of West Georgia. In 2012, I will graduate and be a certificated teacher in the State of Georgia. I once heard a wise professor state, "You cannot teach what you don't know," and what a wakeup call that was for me. That is why I took my studies seriously and took time to read more and learn things that I didn't know before. My reading skills may not have been where I would like them, but I had to work hard to get here. I want to be the kind of teacher that will have a positive flow of energy about every subject I teach. I want to be the kind of teacher that can give students a fair opportunity to learn and make learning meaningful and lifelong.

I enjoy spending time with my parents and being a blessing to them. My dad is no longer on drugs, as a matter of fact he is active in the church. I love my dad so much in spite of the past. I have no bad feeling towards him and we talk just about every other day. My stepmom is also no longer on drugs and become a hard working woman. I have been inviting her to church with me, but because of her work, she's not been able to make it. I believe that she really wants to come. My mom has been off drugs for years, and has no desire to go back to them. She is also married. Praise God they are all doing much better and I love them so much. I thank God for them. I also spent time with my mom and siblings in Atlanta, I enjoyed it. I am waiting on the day when I am able to show my parents a better life. I am going to retire them all, if they want. They wouldn't have to work another day in their lives.

I love giving my testimony because through it I can see the hand of God on His people and watch Him deliver them. The Bible helps us to understand that we overcome by the word of our testimony. I am waiting on God to take me higher in my next level in life. I have discovered I am somebody and I am destined for greatness no matter what people have said or may say. Some people have said that I wouldn't make it and would be nothing in life, but my God always shows up and proves that His words don't return to Him void.

Revelation 12:11 KJV

"And they overcame him by the blood of the lamb; and by the word of their testimony; and they loved not their lives unto death."

I know that God is going to do great things in my life. I believe God is going to take me places that I never thought I would go. Pastor Joel Osteen once said, "Whatever your dreams are, know this God wants to do more. His plan for you will surpass anything you've ever imagined."

Whoever thought that this little black kid from LaGrange would be an author one day? Whoever thought that little Fredrick would be the man he is today and the person who has accomplished so much in life? Whoever thought that one day I would be a teacher and share my life story with millions of people? God has really blessed me more times than I have deserved and I'm thankful for that.

I share my experiences to show people that there is a God and they are not alone in this thing we call life. If He can do it for me, He can surely do it for you.

Receiving Jesus Christ

If you don't know Jesus and would like to receive him as your Lord and savior I would like for you to say this little prayer with me:

Father God, I come to You today and ask You to forgive me of all my sins. Father, I believe in my heart that Jesus Christ is the Son of God and that He died on the cross for my sins. So, I confess with my mouth Jesus as my Lord and savior. So Father I accept You and ask You to come into my heart and save me. Amen!

You have just said this prayer and if you believe it, you are a new person in Christ Jesus. You are not the same person that woke up and got out of bed this morning.

John 3:16-18 NIV

16"For God so loved the world that he gave his one and only Son, that whoever believes in him shall not perish but have eternal life. 17For God did not send his Son into the world to condemn the world, but to save the world through him. [18]Whoever believes in him is not condemned, but whoever does not believe stands condemned already because he has not believed in the name of God's one and only Son.

Reflections

Discuss how you go about setting goals.

The Five Steps

There are five steps I want to share with you. These are steps that I've applied and continue to apply to my life even as I am writing this book. Following these steps, you can encourage and motivate in more ways than one. If you are trying to come out of a storm, catch a break with your finances, break a generational curse or just trying to better your life, then I would like to challenge you to apply these steps in your life. Use what you can and set aside what you can't use.

1. Faith:

When I began attending church, I realized that I couldn't do anything without the Lord's help. From those days forward, I began to trust in the Lord Almighty and depend on Him like never before. Paul states in the Bible that, "Faith is the substance of things hoped for and the evidence of things unseen." (Hebrews 11:1) With that being said, you must have faith in the Lord and yourself. Faith will make things work for your good. So believe.

2. Seek a Mentor:

Most of the time people think a mentor is the person who provides money but that's not the case. A mentor is not necessarily someone who provides you with money, but someone who provides you with something much more valuable than money. A mentor will spend time with you. We all have received money and spent it on something and we will receive more money and spend it again. My point is that money will come and go but *time* is something that you can never get back and this is why time with a mentor is important.

You can have a mentor for different reasons in your life. I didn't mention this earlier but I remember my first mentor, his name was Kevin Cain. I was in the eighth grade and I didn't realize it then but a mentor was something I needed. But one thing I can remember is that Mr. Cain never gave me any money. But Mr. Cain gave me something more important, he gave me time. If I can remember correctly, every Wednesday Mr. Cain came to my school to have lunch with me. When I think about the all the times he came just to see me, I really feel thankful because he didn't have to do it but he did.

A mentor is not always appreciated for his or her time. That's why I would like to take the time to thank all the mentors I have had and for the ones I currently have. They all have shared with me something far greater than money. They will forever be remembered for spending time with me when I thought no one cared for me. Now, Mr. Cain wasn't that mentor that I called up and asked to be my mentor, but this is a perfect example of how one person can make a difference.

Whatever you are trying to do in life, seeking a mentor is a wise decision. Do not be afraid if at first there is an ignored call or unreturned e-mail because I am a firm believer that everything happens for a reason. Hear the Lord and follow your heart. I promise that you will find that the mentors who can give you the tools to go to the next level.

3. Speak Life

If you don't take anything else from this book, please listen to what I have to say here. I've learned the power of praying and speaking life into my future. The Bible states that the tongue can bring death or life and I refuse to speak death. In other words, what you say about yourself or to your future that will come to pass whether it's good or bad. For example, if you say, "I'm not smart or I can't do anything right." Then guess what? You won't be smart enough and you want be able to do it. Start telling yourself, "I am smart and I can do it." The Bible says that, "I can do all things through Christ who strengths me." (Philippians 4:13) So speak life and not death, look in the mirror every day and tell yourself that you are somebody and you can do all things. Never again will you speak badly about yourself.

Let me show you how it works. One thing that I have incorporated into my life is a daily confession. A daily confession is basically a written prayer that you declare over your life every day. In my latest daily confession, I declared that I will receive unexpected checks in the mail and that there is money with my name on it. Would you believe me when I tell you that in a month's time of repeating my confession I received five unexpected checks in my mailbox? That is the power of prayer and speaking life.

While at Gordon College I posted sayings or quotes on my dorm room walls that spoke life into my future. Quotes like, "Fredrick Bailey will be a billionaire" or "Fredrick Bailey will be successful." People asked me why I wrote my quotes in third person and I simply told them that people will come in my room and read what's on my wall and when they read my quotes they would be saying, "Fredrick Bailey is a Billionaire and Fredrick Bailey will be successful." Simply put, people were helping me speak life into my destiny. Even people who really didn't like me would speak life into my destiny by reading my quotes. So I dare you to write down some quotes, in third person, and let people help you speak life.

4. Have a Plan

After talking to Mr. Cofield one afternoon, he showed me a notebook that contained his dreams and goals about his nonprofit organization, Make A Child Smile Foundation. This foundation was started because of the Cofield's passion to help children who had a disadvantage in life.

His notebook also contained other things that he wanted to see happen in his life. He encouraged me to do the same and I did just that. I started to look deeper into my future and I would hear him say, "Don't go and get ready, be ready" and that spoke volumes to me. So, I encourage you to do the same. This is something that I have also implemented with other young people. God blesses a man or woman with a plan, so always have a plan. I call my notebook the "Dream Book."

This is what you need to do: Get a regular three ring binder, page protectors, paper, and tab dividers. In your dream book you could have everything that you envision for yourself. For example, in my dream book I have the following:

1. The meaning of my name, Fredrick, and it means, "Peaceful Ruler." It's no coincidence that I always enjoy being the leader or taking on leadership roles. Even my middle name, Renaldo means "ruler" so every time some call my name they are calling me ruler but I like to joke around say king instead.

2. My biography. It explains who Fredrick Bailey is, what I've accomplished, and what I wish to do in the future.

3. A list of my short and long term goals. (But make sure that they are realistic and reachable!) Also try to break your goals down into mini-goals, it will help you to track and measure your progress.

4. Daily confessions (which are in third person just in case someone else reads it!)

5. A budget to properly manage my finances. It will help so I can save more money and not over spend. I have to remember that my needs come before my wants. I also have a breakdown of how much it will cost me to run my own business because you never know who will stop and ask how much it costs to do what it is I want to do. Remember what I stated earlier, "You don't have time to go get ready, BE READY!" You may never get another opportunity like that again.

6. Pictures. I have pictures from magazines and the internet of things that I dream of or have a desire of getting. For example, you may want a Mercedes Benz, so I would find a picture of it, cut it out, and it place it in dream book. All pages in my dream book are placed in a clear page protector.

7. Quotes. I have a list of inspirational quotes in the back of my dream book. Whenever I have days where I'm in need of encouragements, I grab my dream book turn to the back of it and read my inspirational quotes.

This list is just a few things I have in my notebook. Our visions and dreams will be different so I might have things in my notebook that applies specifically to me and yours will apply specifically to you. Get a notebook and watch how your mindset and outlook about your dreams will change.

5. Have a Budget

I mentioned this earlier as one of the seven things I have in my dream book but if a dream book isn't for you I would still invite you to have a budget. My family and friends know that I try to save money any way I can and don't spend my money on just anything without putting some thought into it. They all call me cheap but I tell them that I'm frugal there is a difference.

Because I don't want to struggle financially, I've learned how to manage a budget. You may be thinking "how can I make a budget when I don't have a job or any type of income?" If you can remember I didn't always have a job or income either, but there are many ways for you to have make earnings. I sold candy but I wouldn't advise you to sell it in school. I have cut grass, run errands, etc. There are ways to make income but you have to go out and find a way regardless of how young or old you are.

Along with the five steps I have given you, I would like to ask you two questions and ask that you really put some thought into it. These questions will help you to identify your skills and interests. There are millions of people working 9-5 jobs that they don't enjoy. I have always heard the most important times in a person's life are: when they are born, and when they discover their calling and purpose. At the age that you are right now, you have to think of two important questions

Two Questions to Ask Yourself

1. What comes easy to me?

Think about why people compliment you. I believe that everybody has one or two things that are easy to them, but harder for someone else. People might even say that you're strange or creepy because you have an extraordinary and unique gift. Can I share a secret with you? People are really admiring your special skills they lack. It may not be something profound or deep; it can be a common activity like planning small events, organizing and cleaning very well, or cooking great meals.

Sit down and think about this question. Focus on what comes to mind and write it down. Once you have thought about this answer ask yourself, "How can I use this to make income for myself and enjoy what I'm doing?"

Thoughts _____

_____
_____
_____
_____
_____
_____
_____
_____
_____

2. What could I do for the rest of my life even if I didn't get paid for doing it?

Think about what you love to do regardless of the money. You love it so much that money really doesn't matter. Imagine the job you hate and then imagine that job you would absolutely love to do. Think about having a great time making money from whatever you like doing. Isn't it a great feeling? Most successful people don't talk about the money part; they talk about how much they love their work. If you fall in love with your work, money will take care of itself. So create another list and write down what you can do for the rest of your life for free.

Thoughts

Notes

I've learned from reading this book that…

I was motivated to do... And why...

This book changed my life because…

For books and media resources or to schedule the author for speaking engagements, contact:

Fredrick R. Bailey

P.O. Box 1858

LaGrange, GA 30241

Phone: 678-736-4177

Internet: Fredrickbailey.com

Email: fredrick@fredrickbailey.com

If this book is in your possession, I would like to ask that you send me an email to the email address above to indicate what part of the world you're located.